VERSES

OF

STARS

Verses of Stars

EVAN KANDAPAN

Acknowledgments

In this journey of creating this collection of poetry, I have been blessed with the support and encouragement of many wonderful individuals whom I would like to express my gratitude to.

First and foremost, I express my gratitude to the Almighty God without whose blessings I could not have come this far. The completion of this book would not have been possible without the help of a large number of people whose name may or may not be listed here.

I am grateful to my parents and my brothers Nillu and Elu for their love, blessings, support and trust in me. I express my gratitude to my dearest friends for always believing in me and encouraging me constantly.

I would like to express my heartfelt gratitude to the members of Notion Press for their cooperation in the process of publishing my dream book. I am forever grateful for this opportunity.

Author's Note

Following the words of Paul Engle who said- "Poetry is boned with ideas, nerved and blooded with emotions, and held together with the tough, delicate skin of words", I begun writing poems to express the emotions and thoughts accumulated over the years. At first, it seemed like an expression of my inner thoughts, but the more I write the more I realise that there are souls who can relate to my poems. So, I kept taking inspiration from every little thing around me and turned them into poetry.

I enjoy reading fictional and non-fictional literature for recreation. I have continuously taken inspiration from the writings of Keats, Yeats, Sylvia Plath, Angelou, Gulzar and many more eminent personalities.

I find writing as the most beautiful way to escape reality for I think that I have complete control over it unlike any other things in this uncertain life. I can create any story I want, a whole new universe and I can make the Gods fall in love with me. But most importantly, it works as a pretty good mirror, able to reflect one's emotions. I would want the readers to use my poems to understand their own emotions.

Evan Kandapan

Contents

1. Dear Stranger

2. Love Poem

3. The day we met

4. Is this love?

5. First light of sunshine

6. Tastes like home

7. Distance between us

8. Peace

9. Heaven

10. December stars

11. Seasons of a lifetime

12. Trapped

13. Escape

14. Rain

15. Letter

16. Song in a world of chaos

17. Gift

18. Will you rescue me?

19. You and I

20. Poet's journal

21. Villain

22. Magic

23. Favourite Song

24. When you walked into my life

25. Clouds of your sky

26. December Love

27. Prize

28. Puzzle

29. Broken stars on your lips

30. Looking for you

31. Brave or cursed

32. Poetic love

33. Two Forevers

34. Second Chance

35. Love with a time stamp

36. It's still you

37. Scars

38. Moonchild

39. Unloved

40. Silhouette of memories

41. Death

42. Fooling humans

43. Heartbreak

44. Void

45. Blue hour

46. Homeless

47. Burning down thoughts

48. Violence

49. Favourite Incomplete Wish

50. Museum of Thoughts

51. Burden of Heartbreak

52. Sweet Poison

53. Half-heart

54. Cursed for eternity

55. Worth dying

56. Pain or Poetry

57. Vibes

58. Incomplete story

59. How it feels to love her

60. Reason

61. Chaos and poetry

62. Poet with a broken heart

63. Strangers

64. You're not Mine

65. Door

66. It is just a break

67. Unwanted ending

68. Love is a myth

69. Nostalgia

70. Courage

71. Broken things can be perfect too

72. Healing

73. Gold and stardust

74. I found love in you

75. Magic

76. The great conjunction

77. Half-a-poet

78. A spoonful of stardust

79. Write about you

80. Elixir

81. Resurrect

82. Universe

83. Poetry of moon and stardust

84. Rise and fall

85. Tuesday

86. Love can never be unconditional

87. Empty canvas

88. Butterflies

89. Sunset

90. My soul asks more of you

91. Dinner

92. Saviour

93. November

94. Resembling the Universe

95. Wild Love

96. Memorable Name

97. Irreplaceable Place

98. Hope

99. You make me whole

100. Home

101. Reality and Love

102. Irrational Love

103. Anomaly

104. Showpiece

105. 10,000 years

106. Gentle Love

107. I am an Island

108. Another Universe

109. Bonds I no longer chase

110. Abundant Love

111. Habit

DEAR STRANGER

Dear Stranger,
As a lover, you do stupid mistakes,
you offer the biggest piece of your heart
without asking anything in return,
you lose yourself trying to
vibrate the same as their world,
you get ready to jump off a cliff
without any parachute
or dive into the deepest ocean
without any oxygen,
you give second chances
as if breaking hearts isn't a crime to you,
you beg for a love you think you deserve
that isn't worth chasing or never will be.

when people leave you
chasing after a barren land and dead stars,
don't follow them
because it won't take long for them to realize
that you were the star they ran from,
and soon they will try to come back
knowing the stardust in you
can heal the broken heart
and soul too.

LOVE POEM

On a sleepless night,
my stares travelled to your eyes
and the stories it hid
and in one of those stories
I saw a love
that chased after us
for it had your name next to mine;
I also saw a picture
of the time we spent together,
the rain we danced in,
the ocean we dived into,
the sky we kissed under,
and the stars we gazed at;
and when your eyes shut me out
for the umpteenth time,
I put them in a love poem
and let the world see it.

THE DAY WE MET

Something boiling inside,
a fire of some sort,
so fierce that it destroys things
that comes in its way,
and the memories stuck
on the walls of my heart
begs me to rip out an opening
except the memory of the day we met,
for the day found a light within me
that saved me from ruining my heart,
the happy ending I saw in your eyes
and the forever you spoke with words
might disappear some day,
But the day we met would never
fade out of my memories.

IS THIS LOVE?

Early morning breeze
sending a wave of chills to the flaky epidermis,
blood rushing through the veins
as if the body is on fire;
the dead pieces of heart feasting on my chest,
and the tiny drops of sweat quenching its thirst;
am I dying or just falling for you?

your smile is so contagious,
and your skin is drawn with the same sand dust
the Greek goddesses were once made of;
your hazy eyes speaking their own language,
yet the soldiers in my heart drop their swords
and the demon surrenders himself

is this love at first sight?

like the one in movies and novels.

is this love at all?

FIRST LIGHT OF SUNSHINE

A mundane restlessness
in the shades of monochrome
is all I can picture now,
and in it I'm drowned
in the pool of your thoughts,
where my existence
lies on your lips
and your smile
heals the cracks in my heart,
where your touch
tames the demons within me
and your heart makes a home for me.

I'm more alive with you
for you're the first light of sunshine
in my lousy dusk of pain.

TASTES LIKE HOME

When the darkness folds
and clouds shimmer amongst
the sparks of the little stars,
breathe me deep into
the corners of your body
and wait for me to find my way
through the edges,
and as I leave your body,
the chaos within you rises with me
and takes over me,
I tighten my grip around your neck
and pulled you towards me,
close enough for our lips to collide,
mine smells like cigarette
and yours tastes like home.

DISTANCE BETWEEN US

When my imaginations
reduce the miles between us
bringing our hearts closer
where I can hide my sorrows
in your collarbone
and you can print your smile
on my forehead,
and our souls entangling
on the sheet of constellations
as our skins seep freckles of stardust
making us two most important entities
in the universe,
and when my imaginations fade away,
I fill the distance between us with words.

PEACE

The thing about
offering pieces of my heart to the strangers
in exchange for stories
is that my heart got crowded
with tales of different language,
fables of different symphony,
and for someone who was homeless for ages
my heart became home
to rose stains of weeping eyes,
to bated breaths of shivering lips,
to dust trails of grieving heart,
and to broken compass of a disowned soul,
and before I realised
my heart was more deranged than the miserable world,
but you entered with an envelope
full of hope, love and words,
hope that brought sunshine,
love that healed me,
and words that I spill on paper
to say to the world that
 you're the peace to my chaotic heart.

HEAVEN

Wrapped up in a gold sheet
under a blue ridden sky,
As I tried to ink down
verses of poems on your frigid skin,
I heard the universe
whispering in my ears the songs of love,
and when your warm breaths
laid down the summer on us
water drops at the edges of our silhouettes
shone due to the lights
bouncing off the clouds
that hanged above us,
and when your heartbeat
raced to the top of the heaven
the words left my heart
to draw a question on your soul
and it answered back
as the touch of your soul
unlocked the cloud gates
that rained down heaven on us.

DECEMBER STARS

There's only infinity
between our universes,
yours constantly trying to soak you in,
and mine whispering in my ears
that I can't have all of you,
I can't have your
soft limbs soaked in a tea cup,
or the summer mornings
at the corner of your lips,
or the slices of sky
falling off your hazel eyes
or the frosty winter
at the tip of your nose.

So when the december stars told me,
"poetry and love are alike"
I wrote poetries
with the words that smells like you,
and the pauses that mimics you,
and when they ask me
what do I want for Christmas,
I reply, "A pinch of love,
a little of magic
and more of you."

SEASONS OF A LIFETIME

When I hold you in my arms,
You lay down **Spring** on my body
and the demons come to life again;
and when **Summer** arrives
between the sheets of our skin,
love flows from your veins to mine;
and before darkness eats me up,
you **Rain** down stars on me;
I shed layers
to the words of your love poems
waiting for my body to change from pink to red to brown
as if **Autumn** arrives early for me;
and my soul stands still when I'm with you
like rusty hours of a **Winter** morning.

Oh Love, when I unmask
the depth of our love
I visit **Seasons** of a lifetime,
again and again.

TRAPPED

I have you trapped
within the boundaries of my mind,
sitting still in the middle of
every spark of ideas
kindled to be molded as poems,
and you don't rush out of this chaos
as if you owe me
to fuel this spark inside me
until I flush out those words
for the universe to see.

And when I do,
all the poems have traces of us
from top to bottom
as if a part of me
is trapped inside my mind, with you.

ESCAPE

Thrown out of a place called home,
he fell down in a pit
of abandonment,
a space devoid of
any muse, magic or memories,
one that turns souls to grey ashes
in which glitters
the sins of the world,
one where a cry for help
is lost amongst the screams
of countless prisoners of fate,
staring at the inevitable end
and waiting to be swallowed by the hole
she offers a hand for him,
a hand that smells like rainbows
and hope written all over it,
a hand that he can grab
to rise out of the death bed,
a hand that can lead him
to a place called escape.

RAIN

I see flowers dripping off the tree
like pain peeled off my skin,
water flowing down the roof
like stardust laid on me,
I hear birds singing
like my heart does around you,
I see the weather painting shades
like you do on my blank canvas
I smell the soil exuding love
like your silhouette emanates on me.

Oh Love!
The rain always reminds me of you.

LETTER

Laying on a flower sheet
under the clouds of stardust
I soak my letter in love
with a pinch of tears
on it's edges,
I write French phrases
about the tales of
moon falling in love with you,
and the nightmares of
the demons waging war against me,
I write about hope
in the corners of hell,
and thunderstorms
in the streets of silver city,
I write about you and me,
also our chaotic reality.

And every letter from me
is a piece of my heart meant only for you.

SONG IN A WORLD OF CHAOS

Sometimes,
I listen to a random song
and when it's over
few lines get stuck in my mind
and I keep humming
the same lines over and over again
while hoping the words
to rearrange themselves
in a shape that resembles you
and the tunes
to imitate your voice,
and at night
lying awake on my bed,
when I listen to the song,
I inject parts of me to it
until the universe
makes it our song.

Because I believe you and I are a song
in a world of chaos,

GIFT

If I was ever to
give you something,
I'd find a box and stuff it with
summer mornings, and winter nights,
sunsets and silver sands,
butterflies and shimmering stars.

I'd cram the box with
sunflowers to heal your heart,
rainbows to paint your soul,
and poems to fulfill your body.
because you deserve
a universe in a box
that fits into your bedroom.

WILL YOU RESCUE ME ?

As I am lost
somewhere between
Adam's world and Eve's world
with a bag full of thoughts,
ones that I wish to tell you,
I fail to recite the poems for you,
or sing the song for you,
and the words come out wrong too,
because this place is killing my words
more than it's killing me,
so before I am out of all the words
to tell you that I love you
will you come to rescue me?

YOU & I

The quest for romanticism
has made people forget who they are,
and most are cursed with an urge
to find love in the teardrops of a cloud,
or in the ink of a scarred moon,
in the flowers inside a diary,
or in rainbows of the sky,
and in search of a forever
people are often blinded
with lust and falsity
bled by the demon,
forcing people to end up
strangers with distasteful memories.

And I've seen people meet,
become 'Us' for a while
and then drift apart later,
so I want us to be
"You & I" until the end.

POET'S JOURNAL

On some salty evenings,
when the fireflies
rose out of your vintage skin,
and the half-asleep eyes
birthed stars of immortal kind,
I untangled words from your hair
that survived
heartbreaks,
and eclipses,
but none of those letters
took me to the last page
where your stories resided.

And for so many nightfall
I couldn't decipher you
because I was never a poet,
but you were a poet's journal.

VILLAIN

History taught us that
not many of us are brave enough
to think ourselves
as the villain in our story,
all we do is take the easy choice
and blame everything on destiny,
but when he loved her against fate
with a tiny bit of hope
and a whole lot of everything to lose,
not once the hesitation kicked in
and when he was half a breath
between killing and being dead,
he chose to be the first,
he was ready to be the villain
who burns the world down
to get what belongs to him
or be a monster
who wages war against gods
to steal her from fate.

MAGIC

Flowers that grows
on your hair,
rainbows that bends
at the corner of your lips,
stars that shine the brightest
through your eyes,
the moon that saves you
when darkness hunts,
the sky that offers stardust
when your skin turns pale,
and the universe that turns pink
when you fall in love,
I've seen them all.

And If it wasn't for you how would I know
that there's magic in the universe?

LYRICS TO YOUR FAVOURITE SONG

It's poetic
when someone remembers
the lyrics to your favourite song
or exactly knows the emotion
that has driven you to
think about them for the whole day,
and how they've become the antidote
for all the dark and depressing thoughts
you stacked up while chasing shadows,
when they become listener
to all your vulnerable conversations
and knows what keeps your soul alive
or what hurts your heart the most,
when they become
your warm cuddles
your safe haven,
and your home,
all in one.

WHEN YOU WALKED INTO MY LIFE

I waited for so long,
and the stars, the raindrops and the withered leaves
chummed up with me,
until you walked into my life
with the biggest grin on your lips,
and stardust on your skin,
you didn't bring butterflies with you,
nor did you make my heart skip a beat,
you didn't bring rainbows with you,
nor did you paint my soul,
instead you brought stories with you,
and every inch of my body felt that,
you brought clouds with you,
and every bit of my soul was wet,

You stared into my eyes
and told me that you were looking for me since a decade,
whispering my name as if it was a spell,
and when you found me you unzipped your skin to offer me
some hope, love and a whole lot of magic.

And I was done with sad stories
the moment you walked into my life.

CLOUDS OF YOUR SKY

On some days,
I ask for clouds of your sky, not the stars or the moon,
clouds that doesn't rain,
but the ones having lightning within it,
capable of causing a thunderstorm
or start a soul-consuming fire,
the flames of which
melts the flesh from my body
exposing calm air to the poems
that are glued to the bones,
meant to be hidden from the universe,
and I don't scream standing in that fire,
I just smile looking at the poems
following the clouds back to your sky
to stay there forever.

DECEMBER LOVE

Sometimes I wonder,
Is love strange from the beginning
or we make it like this
with our complexities?

I think of love as a feather
resting at the tip of our heart,
but we keep adding things to it
without realising that
some day the weight of this love
would be too big for us
and we wouldn't be able
to carry them anymore.

so I hope
love would be like december-
full of moments of peace,
trails of laughter,
kinder days and festive nights.

PRIZE

The world that we know
is divided into good and evil,
right and wrong,
heaven and hell,
and for centuries
we're taught to follow the ways of the heaven;
but in the never ending debate
of destination and journey,
my head tilts in the direction of hell
which urges one
to get more laughter and freedom,
more light and hope
in the journey of love
without worrying about the end
which is uncertain since the inception of time;
and for once in life,
I'd rather have you in the journey
through the dark tunnels of life
than win you as a prize at the end of it.

PUZZLE

When I found a broken half of a
star, I seek the other half diving
deep inside her skin, for I know
that, everything that falls apart or
disappear from the universe, finds
shelter in her heart.

The universe cries out loud at
times to be complete again, to be
beautiful again, but without any scars.

She makes the whole universe
gaze only at her, as she has the
missing pieces of the puzzle that
completes the universe.

BROKEN STARS ON YOUR LIPS

The universe abandoned me
for a sin I committed
as I stole stars from the sky
and adorned them on your skin,
since then, I have been missing out
on the magic of the universe.

So, every night I run back to you,
for I know that It is blissful
to taste broken stars on your lips.

LOOKING FOR YOU

The universe doesn't seem to realise
but you're out there exploring the horizon
while I'm unwillingly rooted
in one of the rings of Saturn.
I can stretch out my fingers,
but what for?
It isn't enough
to touch your star dusted skin,
and there's just space between us,
so little yet so thick.

I hid pieces of me inside you,
hoping that a part of me
will always belong to you,
while I wait for rest of my body
to turn into dust
and float into the empty sky
looking for home,
looking for you.

BRAVE OR CURSED

Do you ever think
how foolishly brave are the souls
who decides to save heart for someone
who doesn't manifest forever in their eyes?
Every day, I try to look into
tons of pairs of eyes
to pick out truths from the ocean of lies
they carry to receive love
that lasts only a moment
as if they're afraid of
walking miles with one person,
so they hide the fear
by leaking lies out of eyes
that they're eternally cursed
to never be in a forever love;

and I often wonder
which side I fall in
the foolishly brave or the eternally cursed?

POETIC LOVE

Have you ever fallen in love
so hard and fast
that you forgot what song makes you happy?
and all you want to do is
mend the lyrics of the song
to mirror the person
whose gaze seep through your soul
to ignite a desire for a hand
that slides between the fingers
and offers a chance at infinite soft touches,
something that stops your body
from shedding skin every night
to match the shade the world wants you in
but now there's one
who loves the unfiltered you-

so, have you ever fallen in love
with someone who's more song than a person?

TWO FOREVERS

I don't sense any emptiness in me,
probably the reason for it is
that many seek one forever
in their whole lives
while I've found two forevers in you.
One 'little forever'
where you and I are one today
and another 'infinite forever'
where you and I have countless memories
for tomorrow.

SECOND CHANCE

Living in a world
where relationships end in unsatisfying ways everyday,
I stood still while the world around me kept moving,
changing between days and nights
days filled with google photos reminders where I smiled,
and nights embedded with trips down the nostalgia tunnel;
with each journey
I lost a piece of me
and was on the verge of turning to dusts
until you met me
where day and night meets,
and there I was begging for my pieces
to be whole again,
to be with you,
to take another chance with life,
cause you make me want to
enjoy my life again.

LOVE WITH A TIME STAMP

The world slowed down
when the clouds of pandemic
rained down on it
and it stopped vibrating with the frequency
that resonated with the hearts of billions,
soon the space between the vibrations
got filled with distance
forcing the souls to drift away,
but during a time like this
I sneaked behind the curtains of a dream
where I found you,
and tried to turn that dream into a reality
believing that even from miles across the world,
it is possible to love,
and so I did,
with every inch of my heart
and I would
till the end of our journey
for I want to show the world that
A love with time stamp isn't necessarily a lesser love.

IT'S STILL YOU

Lifetime ago
it was you,
who wanted to know my favourite colour
and the poems I read at night,
it was you,
who wanted to listen to the sound of my laughs,
and who showed me
the language of love can be
long walks down the beach,
star-gazing in your balcony,
and dancing in the rain;

maybe we got lost
while chasing the secrets of the universe,
but we're still part of
the beautiful story I stumbled upon,
you still know how to
un-hurt my scars
and make me write poems about us,
and just like that
lifetime later
it's still you.

SCARS

I always wondered
why my scars never spoke
the language of hatred
until I realised the scars are in love with you
cause you still live in it
carrying the burden
of gate-keeping the monster
that wants to rip apart the scars
and come out of my body stealing
memories, dreams, hope
and words-
everything that makes me write,
so, the monster has to stay inside
and be a nourishment for my soul
till the day I decide to write
for me and for the monster.

MOONCHILD

I thought someday a portrait of mine
would appear on the moon,
a silhouette
wrapped around in perfect lines
and filled with shades of rainbow,
but here I am,
a broken canvas
with painted colours one over the other
without any blend,
and when I see moon today
I see reflections of a painting of mine
brushed with nothing but red,
a sign of me heading down
the path of pain
while in pursuit of happiness,
tonight the moon is me,
and I am the moon.

UNLOVED

For years,
casted as unloved
amongst the few fortunate ones,
one gets into
many lives, many heavens, many hells,
but temporary stays everywhere
as if they rescind
the fibres of one's body,
that was put into the world
to carry the curse of the loved ones,
however,
there are far too many souls now
ready to rebel against
the one being who pretends to be almighty
or the ones who believe in his existence.

SILHOUETTE OF MEMORIES

Being stuck in awe of the bloom
that takes shape to be a flower,
sometimes we forget
about the haunting wreckage
that is destined to follow,
as if the bittersweet memories
unlike any other time
would change the course of fate
and unlike any other day
wouldn't slip out of the hands,
and unlike any other reality
would hold the souls together,
but we know that
fate wouldn't change course,
hands wouldn't always hold,
and souls grow apart,
and the only thing that remains
is the silhouette of memories.

DEATH

Woke up burned by the fires
of the fights between
the angels and the demons
inside my soul,
and amongst this chaos of detachment
and of unrequited love,
the soul feeds on pieces of my own heart
leaving me clueless
as to why I breathe death
even if I only consume
ice-cream and poetry
and the quest for
the final embrace of a graveyard
ends at the ocean floor
where I sink into a world of rest and silence.

FOOLING HUMANS

At times my chest gets filled
with fragments of memories and conversations,
with pieces of dreams and anecdotes,
and with thoughts that move around
the edges of the ribcage,
often pinching the heart on its way
and my heart screams your name and death,
leaving me overwhelmed
by the beauty of its bliss and ache,
so I try to fool my heart
with the words of a Jane Austen novel
like the stars do
with the humans,
cause on some nights,
the stars move places
to fill the void to fool humans
that the stars never die.

HEARTBREAK

When I met you,
you were still trying to fix the cracks in your heart
with the potion of bitterness,
and it took me eons to look for a way to translate my soul
until one day you spoke the same language as me,
as happiness spells as silence
and love spells as heartbreak.

It took you days to open up to me,
weeks for me to fall for you,
and months for us to save each other
from our own emptiness,
but there was too many gaps in your past
and every time you peeked into those empty spaces
trying to fill that void
you lost another piece of you,
and before your heart turned into a black hole,
before your body turned into a graveyard,
you gifted me a painless heartbreak,
that didn't get lost or reeked of death.

VOID

The hollow void in my room
and of my heart,
echoed the constant throbbing of bones
against the shivering skin
and I kept waking up
as if my eyes were slaves
to the symphony created
by the love-ridden bones
and the cold waves of a friday night.

I try to get rid of this cold skin
to see if warmth exists inside me,
but there is too much dust of loneliness
to see through,
and the poetic parts in me fall apart,
throwing words to the walls,
"how every one of us deserve love,
how we always look for new songs,
new books, new places,
and new people to fall in love with."

BLUE HOUR

I don't see the spark in your eyes,
ones that you've painted with nightmares,
and I don't write poems
to make you stop and stare at dreams too,
you no longer smile at the camera
and I'm out of shades to draw you one,
you have lost music to our dance
and I let the universe use filters on us,
you've lost the way back to our home
as I find us in chaotic parallels,
maybe the sunset is also gone,
what we wished our love to be.

And maybe our love has become
the silence before the dawn
where you've fallen asleep
and I haven't woken up yet.

HOMELESS

Often riddled with the question
whether the shooting star
belongs to the sky or the earth,
whether the sand particles
belongs to the ocean or the shore,
I stand here
on threshold of wondering
If I'm allowed in your heart or not
while sending poems your way
to get that nod of approval.

BURNING DOWN THOUGHTS

It hasn't been long since I parched
my heart with thoughts in it,
but the antibodies in me
stopped the flames,
and I still hear the half baked thoughts
crawling on the walls
loud enough to burst my eardrum
yet not ringing the ears
of souls around me,
and when I bleed
smokes come out of it
along with the screams
of "I'm broken"
which I've been hiding from universe,
and I stand in solitude
with an unanswered question-
"Is the leftover thoughts
going to disappear on its own
or do I need to cage them in my body
and burn it down to ashes?"

VIOLENCE

Being afraid of abandonment
I did violence to my own heart,
pushing away pieces
that are easy to love,
and the ones that remains
are addicted to the taste of insanity and grief;
insanity of destroying myself
before anyone else does,
and grief of offering stars to souls
who falls in love with seas,
and with time the heart accumulates
a dark and painful sadness
of not what had not been,
but what would never be,
and now I wait for a miracle to save me
because there isn't enough
acetaminophen in the world
to take away the pain of my heart.

FAVOURITE INCOMPLETE WISH

Forever is such a beautiful lie
where you spend lifetime
looking for people
who understands your soul
without any translation,
and in return, the universe offered you
a heart with mosaic of memories
and banishing you from it,
so you run to someone
who's kind enough
to heal the wounds they never carved,
and when fate intervenes,
everyone wants to skip the part
where you have to
let someone go
but it's not possible, is it?
so you chose to have them as
your favourite incomplete wish.

MUSEUM OF THOUGHTS

It's 3 am
and sleep hasn't been kind to you,
so you decide to turn back time
and break down conversations
you had years ago
trying to re-live that warm sensation
of being loved and treasured,
but to your dismay
all you experience is a cold shiver
piercing through the heart,
a feeling you've tried hard giving up
but failed miserably,
and now your body has become
a museum of thoughts and conversations
where you're stuck forever,
or atleast till someone comes to get you.

BURDEN OF THE HEARTBREAK

For centuries,
humans have stained
heartbreak with dishonesty,
filling vocabulary with pain and grief,
often showing it as a graveyard
where all emotions die,
but little do they know
heartbreak as a remnants of a relationship
can be beautiful too,
if you're loved by the right person,
one who saved you
from your inner demons
and introduced you to a version of you
no one knew existed,
one who offered you
magic and strength
that lasts for an eternity,
and if the ending doesn't define
the depth of such love,
then you can carry
the burden of heartbreak
like she carried the weight of love
for the two of you.

SWEET POISON

The torn pages of a book
that once used to hold
the saddest love story known to heavens,
have rained down
and found their way
to the hearts of a few chosen souls,
who are cursed to carry
the remnants of heartbreaks
belonging to the entire humanity;
and with time
the pages took shape of hope
well dipped in sweet poison
that brings smile to the lips
but kills from inside.

HALF HEART

One half of your heart longs for
the right person
who would never leave your shadows
and the other half knows
that it doesn't happen for you,
the lover in you wants a love
that walks in through the door
and stays with you until the end,
you turn heaven and hell upside down
trying to make it work,
but you constantly got hurt,
and instead of listening to the sane half,
the other half keeps making up stories
and imagining life with them
in exchange for pieces of your heart
and it keeps on doing so
until you run out of pieces to love,
yet you choose to stay with a love,
that breaks you in half,
hoping for the person
to save the other half.

CURSED FOR ETERNITY

When little drops of imagination
rains down on me,
I find myself in a world
where the devil walks among the living souls
with evil in his eyes and divinity in his body,
with a burning face and an immortal skin
as the devil chooses
to search for answers after absconding
the burden of sins of the humanity.

Imitating the Devil,
I inherited the legacy of evil,
that pushed people away from me
so far that no fantasy ever manages
to put me in a place,
where light illuminates
the value of love and affection,
that has continued to hold people together,
but not around me.

And when I open my eyes,
the bruises are back,
for I am cursed for eternity,
just like the devil.

WORTH DYING

An aching heart
carrying the feeling of dying within,
and the sleepless lungs
breathing in oxygen from my sin,
the relentless moon and wicked nights
inflicting fiery pain on my chest,
the smokes I inhale
that's trapping me in an illusion,
yet I see an unheard poetry,
a magical divine,
a skin with stars embedded on it
and lilies on hair,
but the flesh on fire
like a burning cigarette,
a puff of which
takes an ounce from my soul
and replaces it with muse.

I carry the pieces I trade my life for,
and weave them into a poetry
that only resonates your name,
because nothing more than you,
is worth dying for.

PAIN OR POETRY

I tried to steal healing from the ocean
for I was tired of watching
my heart breaking into pieces
every time a person leaves my hand,
and some days my heart aches so much
when I am drinking coffee,
reading poems,
or seeing the sunsets,
It aches so much that it feels physical
as if some limb or bone in my body
is constantly torn apart.

And all that is I am left with is
a broken heart that spills pain,
or poetry,
or both.

VIBES

A scar you are,
a scar like me,
like the one we hide under the freckled skin
covered with poems and songs,
and spaghetti that we eat
for lunch and dinner,
the coffee I poured
into your memory
and few ballads too,
the melodies I sang for you
when we love and unlove
in the same summer,
and in the afternoon
when we tried unscribbling the scars
fate drew a bigger one
that stole you
and my words too.

So now we talk through the vibes
just like the stars in the constellation do.

INCOMPLETE STORY

I know that everyone has a story
that's painful and heartbreaking,
and maybe hidden inside a diary
or in a box underneath the bed,
far away from the people,
waiting for someone to unravel,
just like me,
so the next time you meet someone
ask them about their
incomplete story
and tell yours.

HOW IT FEELS TO LOVE HER

Time has taught me that
no human body with a beating heart
can know how it feels to love her,
to be under the same sky,
and breathe the same air,
she isn't just a thought
to be forgotten,
nor does she a dream
to fade into thin air,
she was unfiltered words, syllabic haiku,
perfect sonnet, immortal ballad,
broken paragraphs, unfinished letters,
beautiful ode, and love poems,
she was a cold breeze and sandstorm,
a gentle rain and cyclone,
a quite spark and wildfire,
she was a fantasy, a miracle,
a magic that the reality couldn't define,
she was a home,
but on the top of a sailing boat,
slowly floating away from the land
where I wait for the waves,
but not for her.
Why?

REASON

If I were a star
I would've loved you
with all my sides,
but something has changed,
as I've suffered enough,
I stood silent
as you go through
all the second chances
I had to offer you.
Even after all this,
the sole reality
is that my body may turn
his back on you
but my soul will always
find a reason to hold on to you.

Because,
the human part of me
is tired of chasing you,
but my soul isn't.

CHAOS AND POETRY

You ripped off my skin
until it was just chaos and poetry :
chaos tearing every atoms
in my body from within,
and poetry exploring the ashes of
melancholic memories.

Atoms of ocean,
of sky, of stars, of you
and memories of days,
of weeks, of things,
of laughter, of pain,
are hidden under my skin.

And I live an ecstasy of love
every time your lips explore
the chaos and poetry.

POET WITH A BROKEN HEART

Over the past few springs,
I have learned to wear my heart on the sleeves,
only to give bits to the people I meet,
and in doing so,
I have seen half of me making it to the end of life,
while the other half keeps chasing after poetry.

I remember when
I asked for magic, love and
poems from the universe,
I was given mirage, heartbreaks
and meaningless words,
so I put on a mask
to live amongst the masks,
to be one of the lies,
to be one of them.

But I'm afraid when the mask falls off,
the world will know that
I'm just a poet with a broken heart.

STRANGERS

The last page of the book that had us, is long gone,
the coffee stains on my skin are vanishing,
the kisses you left on my sweatshirt are fading,
the world we lived in is falling apart,
and the universe doesn't just stand in awe
as we fall out of love
because I've seen the stars unloving the clouds,
one flame at a time.
And the flames of the star
and the clouds are strangers again,
just like us.

YOU ARE NOT MINE

You're not mine,
You have never been mine,
but why do I love you knowing very well
that I'd be hurt in the end?
why do I hold onto our memories
as if they keep us together?
why do I look for you everywhere
when I crave to listen to your voice?
why do I look into your eyes
to find a reality where we can be together?
why do I run to stand beside you
when the whole world abandons you?
why do I become such a fool when it comes to you?
why do I not accept the truth
that some stories are meant to exist in dreams only?
Why do I hold onto you knowing that you're not mine?

DOOR

Everyday feels like a war,
and I keep on losing each one of them,
but the end is never near.
I am always at the front,
holding the same broken shield,
fighting for the same broken heart,
yet death never harms me,
as if I've become a ghost,
lost in some wildest nightmare,
with only a whisper of your silent cries
piercing through my heart.

In that nightmare, I see a void around me,
where the symphony are meaningless sound,
poetries are broken words
and paintings are scrubbed shades.

And so I need a way out of this fractal dimension,
I need a door to reality,
to light, to life,
but mostly to you.

IT IS JUST A BREAK

You brought words with you
and I thought that
this was forever - you, me and poetry.
But all that is left now is
me, poetry and memories of you.
But I never believed it was destined
For me it was just a break,
For me it is just a break.

UNWANTED ENDING

I, full of midnight stories
And You, a song of the murky dawn
Yet, we crossed paths
like it was meant to be.
You said about past lives,
and I was persistent on coincidence,
but we were lucky the stars elucidated.
The night when we laid down
under the redbud tree
in your backyard,
you narrated your past to me
and I recited a few poems.
We talked about love, music and books
and my stupid heart fell for you,
but yours didn't.
My words matched your chords,
but you wanted to explore more skies.
And once again,
the universe whacked me
with an unwanted ending.
Sometimes I wonder
why didn't the stars say something
like it did the day we met.

LOVE IS A MYTH

The worst trick
that the destiny has played on us
is cursing some souls more than others
who wants to look for love,
some gets it while some doesn't,
so they write the definition of love
as they experience for themselves,
truth for some and myths for others;
the idea of love was introduced to me
when grandfather bought flowers for grandma
or when grandma made chai for him every morning,
when dad stays behind to help mom in cooking
or when mom sits at the door waiting for him,
but not everything pass down through genes
for I find myself cursed in love
unaware of the truths,
and so I realise
love is nothing but a myth for me.

NOSTALGIA

I'm still carrying a tiny forever with me
well decorated with
memories of you uttering my name with your lips,
moments where we paused time
and captured our smiles
on a digital canvas,
one that no longer shines
when light falls on it
as if it turns black
like the sky above my head,
which brings nothing but storms
named after persons,
and there's something extremely risky
about such storms,
they arrive unannounced
taking you on a bittersweet ride,
that scratches your scars
but leaves behind a grin of nostalgia
of unending forever,
and a tale of survival to tell.

COURAGE

As I try to sleep through an innocent dream,
I am constantly drawn back to reality
by the songs coming out of a guitar,
where the burning strings
inject flames of emotions
like the faith in magic,
passion for poetry,
and courage to love again.

BROKEN THINGS CAN BE PERFECT TOO

As I have pulled the thread
more than what I needed to,
I cut down the one thing
that kept my thoughts at bay
from blending in with the nightmares,
and now it's harder than ever
to liberate my thoughts
from the box of madness,
one that was originally meant for
the sparkling beads of
red of the passion of the heart,
blue of the rhythm of the poetry,
white of the tenderness of love
and purple of the remnants of dreams,
but now it's all blurry
to find the right kind of bead
to write the perfect poetry,
might as well pick what I touch
to create a poem
and pretend to be a philosopher who says
broken things can be perfect too.

HEALING

I've been up all night
watching bruises on my soul
as if I'm no longer
the hero of my own sloppy poem,
and the only things
that I truly understand
are the language of grief
and the lyrics of the 3AM songs,
of which the later being
the cure in the vastness of the heartaches,
and the music has been
the only recipe for healing.

GOLD AND STARDUST

The consequences
of my partial withdrawal from us,
turned out to be a sloppy poem in the language of grief,
one that has traces of the dusk;
the darkest shade of twilight that stole the space between us,
the dusk with venom that poisoned
the infinite walled reality we were in,
and the only antidote for healing I knew was love
but I was ran out of it,
or atleast that is what the stars told me,
and when I peeked into my own heart
I found multiple cracks in the hourglass
that you had placed the first time we met,
all the stardust in it were covered with ashes,
ashes of the promises I couldn't keep
and the sunsets I walked out of,
I knew I had to fix the hourglass back
with some gold and lacquer
as they do with a kintsugi pot,
and then I realise
maybe
we can be like Kintsugi pot,
once covered with cracks,
but now an alluvium of gold and stardust.

UNTIL I FOUND LOVE IN YOU

I survived in a world
where the void in my heart
was bigger than a black hole,
that ate up the glitters of the sky,
the dusts of the universe,
and the words of the poems,
but at times the love ridden soul of mine
resembled a wild volcano, which flared up
the last ounces of hope and magic
turning my body into just a vessel.

But when fate threw me on a wrong path
it led me to a right destination
where you promised me
forever sunsets to capture,
painted skies to live under,
and shimmering light to rekindle my heart;
And the universe stood still
as you peeled me part by part,
eons after eons,
until I found love in you,
until I found love for me.

MAGIC

I used to scream at the universe
asking to Evanescence everything,
things that sunk my soul
in the ripples of people
vanishing from my life,
things that drained my heart
in a pool of souls,
souls which scarred their sins on my limbs,
leaving behind an asphyxiation
for hope and love,
And then the heaven answered
when you showed up
with a mark of solace on your face,
a taste of life on your lips
and poems inked all over your body,
And the stars witnessed
as I stood in awe of your magic
when you saved me from
being sucked into an abyss.

THE GREAT CONJUNCTION

When the december fog
settles on the wildflowers,
and the celestial gods
are only one-tenth of a degree apart,
when the whole world looks up
to witness the great conjunction,
I see you searching for the pieces
of your heart in a wild unknown,
you are broken and ready to
settle for anything,
just to be able to call something
that only belongs to you,
you have emptied yourself so much
and now there is nothing left,
so I try to fill your void
with ink and words,
with some colourless silence,
but you insist the mystery
of your empty vessel
is too unearthly.

And I say, "there will no longer be
a mystery to your vacant soul
if you just let me put poetry
on top of it."

HALF-A-POET

The November heart of mine
wrapped up in misery shaped fog,
craves for romanticism
in the particles of winter sunlight,
for the chilly dipped clouds
have consumed the warmth of my soul,
sucking out every ounces of love
from my limbs and the veins,
leaving behind words and metaphors
for me to bleed them out
on sheets of paper on a monday morning,
maybe that's how love is mysterious
for I was wordless when I was in love
and now I'm just half-a-poet without it.

A SPOONFUL OF STARDUST

At times,
the scarred soul of mine,
hungry for flesh and blood,
wanted to go out
and find a stranger to love,
but it was hard,
not to fall in love
but to let them in,
cause I was more afraid of them
finding the irreparable damages inside me,
And yet, when I bumped into her
I couldn't help but let her in,
and before I realised,
my heart was covered with band-aid,
a spoonful of stardust,
and a love that heals.

WRITE ABOUT YOU

Sometimes I run fast
hoping to outrun the demon
that is infecting the soul
like some virus without a leash,
making me crave for
vials of poison, death trapped in boxes,
and bruises on my vessel,
sometimes I want to
throw myself at blinding lights,
that can break my skin into parts
and rejuvenate the cells of my body
giving me a new life,
a life where sleepy mornings
and sleepless nights
live on your arms,
And the only thing I want
is to untangle the past
from the pages of my diary
until I find a blank one
to write about you.

ELIXIR

The darkness
that was layered on my heart
and the pain
that was carried in my veins,
made me slave to a ghost,
breathing inside me
only to steal my soul,
but love arrived on time
and I said goodbye
to the rotten layers of my heart,
and with it, the cursed past
that was hunting me.

For all I knew, Love was an elixir
that replaced every curse
with you.

RESURRECT

The broken me,
embracing the dying sun
through the cracks of my heart,
waiting for the summer to burn
the scarred skin of my body,
or the winter to tear me into pieces
until there's nothing left of me,
and when lost
like a spring breeze,
you rained on me
only to drench me
in your magic and love,
and with that magic
I resurrect, as a part of you.

And the cracks in my heart are now
filled with the specks of autumn.

UNIVERSE

The broken me,
embracing the dying sun
through the cracks of my heart,
waiting for the summer to burn
the scarred skin of my body,
or the winter to tear me into pieces
until there's nothing left of me,
and when lost
like a spring breeze,
you rained on me
only to drench me
in your magic and love,
and with that magic
I resurrect, as a part of you.

And the cracks in my heart are now
filled with the specks of autumn.

POETRY OF MOON AND STARDUST

When god blinked,
or clicked his finger
I fell down on a strange land,
and the heart left my chest,
and while I was collecting the words
to fill the hole in my chest,
I saw you walk through
the smoke of the night,
led by the shimmering stars,
that showered stardust on you,
and you were silver
as if the moon painted you
with its own colour.

And it didn't take long
to fall in love with you,
for I was a poet,
and you, a poetry
made of moon and stardust.

RISE AND FALL

Words and hues were glued
into my heart valves,
coiled and tangled,
making the heart skip beats
against the tune of the universe,
and the woeful blend of
letters and colours
that reached the tissues
causing cuts and scars
until you inject love into my veins
that healed my heart.

And you made my heart
rise and fall in sync with the universe.

TUESDAY

Pain is like that monday
which always arrives at a time
when you are struggling to
find the pieces of your heart
once lost when you were in love,
when you are tired scrubbing
the scars off your skin
the so called souvenirs for loving
the wrong person,
when you are begging
the universe to rescue your soul from
the ruins of melancholic memories,
when you are looking
for a way out of a world
where you feel more trapped
than you ever felt safe,

And you are the tuesday
that brought healing to my heart.

LOVE CAN NEVER BE UNCONDITIONAL

For most part of our life,
we chase after an idea of unconditional love,
but I think there exist no such thing,
because everything comes with conditions,
we often want someone to be perfect,
someone that merits our love,
but they're not, they can never be,
no one can ever be.
We put conditions in the way
they influence our existence,
affect our lives,
and nurtures our soul,
so love can never be unconditional.

EMPTY CANVAS

All those nights
sitting under the stars,
I have conversations,
stories,
and secrets
buried under my heart.
At times,
I dig into the heart
to grab the words
and send it to the cosmos,
for I know that
it will return to me
as some wild poetry.

Because the cosmos
made me its pen,
for the world is an
empty canvas,
and millions of stories
still to be inked.

BUTTERFLIES

I remember the butterflies
in my stomach going on a
rampage, feasting on the
pieces of my heart,
until your wildest touch
injects a flame that coursed
through every inch of me,
the soothing fire healed
the torn pieces while
pushing the butterflies away,
so, when you ignited
the fire within,
the butterflies found a way out.

SUNSET

The renaissance cloud,
that captures the smell of the rain
and the colour of the lightning,
throws itself at me,
and the ocean and the stars
deny to take me in
as I become a slave to the sky.

In a world like this,
I surrender myself to your light
to put an end to the rampage
of the floating clouds,
because, You're the calm sunset
to my wild and untamable sky.

MY SOUL ASKS MORE OF YOU

You're just a magician
When you peel off my skin
to move deeper into my bones
leaving trails of your touch,
When you scratch them
with your stubborn fingernails
and You punched them hard.

You keep the wildness in me alive
with your brutal nudge
You're just a magician
and my soul asks more of you.

DINNER

I kept eating regrets and abandonments,
which slid down my throat in abundance
but never made it out of the digestive system
and my body kept draining energy out of my soul
that seemed to get weaker every night,
but on the next morning
I hide my fragile self
behind a smile that hurt
until the day my mother saw through the lie
but she didn't say anything,
however, last night
she cooked dinner for me
which had few hundreds of calories
of healing and love,
and a pinch of hope
for days when the heart is too heavy to carry.

SAVIOUR

Everyone is carrying
the death of a piece of their heart
which loved without any limits,
but now looking for a person
who can be their safe haven
where the nightmares get a voice
and chaos gets accepted,
cause true peace begins
at the hands of a savior who can replace the grave
with a garden of emotions
that draws all kinds of seasons,
the ones you were once deprived of.

NOVEMBER

November shows up
at my glass window
leaving trails of dew drops on it,
and each drop carries
a world of its own
and one such world belongs to you,
you let me in
with the brightest smile
and offered me a place
to be my real self
and in return
all I hope is to have right pieces
that completes your puzzle.

RESEMBLING THE UNIVERSE

At some point in your life,
you see your heart carved,
licked by knives and swords,
as if your heart went on a war of its own
and now screams only of death,
dripping sins and memories of lovers
who moulds your soul
and who breaks your heart,
transforming your body into a mess,
having fragments from the ocean,
from the sky,
the clouds,
the volcanoes,
the living
and the dead,
which is normal
cause if not mess,
how are you going to resemble the universe?

WILD LOVE

Sometimes,
you have many paper cuts
in your heart,
some deep enough to send
tremors in your chest,
but you are unable to name them
until few paper cuts intersect at one point
and a little piece falls out
sending screams of pain
to every inch of your body
as if a curse has been placed on you
by the universe for loving too much,
however, on days like this,
don't forget to wake up from pain
to love the only way you know ;
"wild and without any doubt".

MEMORABLE NAME

For some souls,
who are in never-ending war
with silence,
sometimes, we struggle
to find any combination of letters
to name the kind of feeling
our heart gets constantly feed into
by a single person in the whole universe,
a feeling that no sane mind understands
except us,
and so we remember the feeling
by a name that can stay with us
tomorrow, forever and beyond.

IRREPLACEABLE PLACE

In a world,
where love is often measured
by the number of pictures
you click together,
the number of times
you utter I love you,
or the number of people
talking about your relationship,
I think what lasts forever
are the words
"You're special to me"
for I know that,
fate might steal you from me
or show mercy on us,
but you're always going to be that someone
who is important to me,
who has an irreplaceable place in my heart,
and for whom I'd wage war against gods
to protect.

HOPE

Three hundred and something dead nights,
of writing love note about you,
have fought amongst themselves
and it has lead to
deaths of many yesterdays,
the ghosts of which have tainted
the air of tomorrows
with screams and solitude,
declaring me a loser on both sides
resented by past and future alike,
a traitor with no home
or someone to run back to,
yet, a wild kind of hope
spread over today
wants to take me to all places
beyond yesterday and tomorrow.

YOU MADE ME WHOLE

I wait days picking the words to hold a silence
where I finally found a love like yours,
after spending eons worrying
about ending more than the beginning
so much that I miss out on many adventures;
I felt your aura touching the trauma inside me,
and hope crawled out of my body
and with it- a part of me
that was dead for a millennium,
your love overshadowed the pain I had
and painted me with shades of hope,
and after countless days
I no longer spend nights believing in the false love
for I know that you found me broken
and made me whole.

HOME

When our bodies collided
and the weight of my love
engulfed the weight of your agony,
many soft stars came out of your body
and with it came out the love
that was screaming my name
and my heart jumped out too,
knowing you were carrying the love
I had searched for in my entire existence
the kind of love that makes me vulnerable in your arms
yet invincible against the world,
the kind that pushes away all my sufferings
yet makes me sad in your absence
and in my mind,
my voice mimicked yours
where I told you
that my eyes might be tainted with grief
my arms might be scarred with leftovers,
and my ribs might be knifed with uncertainty
but my heart will always be a home to you
and to your love.

REALITY AND LOVE

Why do everyone believe
that the paradise is at the end,
can't the journey be a little paradise
where no claws of destiny
or the piercing eyes of gods
touches the bubble
of your uncertain yet limited love,
won't the memories be better
than a blank slate
even if they taste bitter-sweet,
we all choose love
but reality chooses only a few of us,
cause on most days
reality and love are contradictory.

IRRATIONAL LOVE

No great love stories started with
someone being rational,
they're often about an impossible person
wanting someone to find them
and take them on a uncertain ride
to seek forever
where hands coloured with misery
are always held by hands full of hope,
and where pieces of heart are rejoiced
rather than getting killed in the name of love,
isn't a love like this nothing more than a fantasy?
But if there is such a love,
It would beat your chest in sync
with the rhythm of your favourite song,
It would transform the sky above your head
into the softest silk to you to warm your soul,
It would build a shrine with all the sins of your history
for you to pray and seek forgiveness,
It would give you strength to fight against the world.

ANOMALY

You showed up in my life
like an anomaly
stealing me from the cycle of monotony
to a place where I found hope,
where your presence feels like poetry
with each words dissecting my soul
into poetic symphonies,
a sum of which makes my heart
not a slave but a refuge
in a safe haven,
where each day,
each night,
each moment,
each memory,
and each heartbeat
becomes You.

SHOWPIECE

The beauty of the love
you scribbled in my heart
might just be an antique showpiece
meant to be stored in a museum now,
but it was once enough
to built a home with your name on it
and fill it with countless memories
like the warmth of your hug
turning my chaos into solace,
the laughter of yours inside my mouth when we kissed,
the strength of your light
saving me from an inescapable night.

10,000 YEARS

Nobody knows exactly
the result of their choices
or have the key
to a tomorrow of what they desire,
however, they must realize
that love is the simplest emotion
and can take you through
the door inside someone's soul
nine out of ten times
and the only time you are locked out of it,
remember the password is
"Love you for 10,000 years"

GENTLE LOVE

Why do we settle with ordinary
when it comes to love?
What if we keep waiting for a love
that is gentle to our heart
yet strong enough to make you feel safe
in the centre of a storm,
the kind that calms your soul
amidst the chaos of the world,
the kind that becomes your safe haven
where you can take refuge when the world abandons you,
the kind that knows your worth
and show it to their actions,
so do not settle until you find such a love.

I AM AN ISLAND

Does God really push people away
or do they leave on their own
seeing the heavy walls of promises
around my heart?
Is this all my doing?
the answers of which
has driven me away
from a world of chaos to a solitude
where no soul recognizes my face,
but one day,
a gaze, so powerful
pierced through my heart
to read the words engraved on the walls
and my reality was no longer a secret,
a reality where I am an island,
merely a pit stops for ships that come and go.

ANOTHER UNIVERSE

The humanly vessel of yours
can't stop the inevitable
and everything might end one day
well short of that forever you desire the most
but I know there won't be a single dent in your heart
for fate can never wash off
the forever written on every inch of your body
that can last at least seven lives,
So, you'll meet again in another universe,
in another timeline,
in entirely different bodies,
and you will have that forever.

BONDS I NO LONGER CHASE

Yesterdays are filled with memories
of standing alongside
unreciprocated, unappreciated
and unrequited emotions
while people walk out on me,
leaving behind their absence for me to fill,
and I did,
with words and letters
turning everything into little stories
where my heart no longer craves them
and doesn't shed tears
when they drift away as some distant symphony
maybe my heart has learned
when to close its door on some bonds,
bonds that I no longer chase.

ABUNDANT LOVE

I love in abundance,
sometimes more than hearts could contain
and as a result,
some love spills out
and falls on bones, muscles and blood,
penetrating into them
to turn them into second home as precaution
if those hearts ever decide
to close its door on my love
for it can hurt them
as much as it can heal them
for love is capable of both
rainbows and storms,
makes some feel safe
while start war against others,
bleeds the sick to find them a cure
or cut open wounds that never closes,
may reshape stories
to change circumstances
and make them embrace life
giving them a story to cherish forever.

HABIT

Of all the things in the world
I don't want to just be
another habit in your life,
I'd rather want you
to dug your way into my core
and set up home within my heart
to seep hope into your body
using arteries,
I'd want to be your 12 minutes talk
to listen to your fleeting thoughts
or be a short stop to your overthinking,
I'd want to be the catalyst
that pushes you away from darkness
and give you strength to take on world again,
I'd want to be the well you drink from
to hydrate your parched soul
or be a lifeboat of survival
when you're about to sink into solitude,
I'd want to be an immortalized moment
in the vast sea of your memories,
I'd want to be your 7 minutes
the time our brain lives to experience
the precious moments about our life
before death consumes us,
I'd rather want to be your story
than just a happy ending.

9 798889 290053